# Dream of Santa

## Haddon Sundblom's Vision

# Dream of
# Santa

*Haddon Sundblom's Vision*

*Staples & Charles*
*Washington, D.C.*

**Acknowledgements**

*Working on this catalogue, and a broader study still in progress, has
been a wonderful visual and intellectual voyage through the myths sur-
rounding Santa Claus, the artistic world of Haddon Sundblom, and the
marketing philosophy of The Coca-Cola Company. Such journeys are
rarely without knowledgeable and thoughtful guides and this was no
exception. Philip F. Mooney and Joanne Newman at the Archives of The
Coca-Cola Company provided total access to the Company's advertising
collections and resources. Their support and encouragement throughout this project has been especially gratifying. Without the interest of
the Coca-Cola (Japan) Company Limited this catalogue would not have
been produced. Without the blessing of Bruce Gilbert of the Merchandise Licensing Department and Michael Ellison of the Legal Division,
both of The Coca-Cola Company, it could not have been produced.*

*The opportunity to try out our ideas about Santa Claus and Haddon
Sundblom at the 1992 convention of the Golden Glow of Christmas Past
society was extremely helpful and we thank Jim Morrison for inviting us.
Dede Schaeffer of Lancaster, Pennsylvania, and Roy and Grace Olsen of
Wayne, Pennsylvania, graciously shared their ideas and collections, while
discussions with Jeffrey Eger of the Thomas Nast Society were very helpful. And finally we are especially grateful to Bill Bateman and Randy
Schaeffer of Reading, Pennsylvania, who carefully reviewed this manu-
script. Their exceptional knowledge of the ephemera of The Coca-Cola
Company and their concern for proper typesetting and editing were
invaluable. Errors, however, remain ours alone.*

——*Barbara Fahs Charles and Robert Staples*

*00 99 98 97 96    9 8 7 6 5 4*

*Produced under the authority of The Coca-Cola Company, owner of the
trademarks COKE, COCA-COLA and the design of the contour bottle.*

*ISBN 0-9634907-0-2*          *Text: Barbara Fahs Charles and J.R. Taylor*
*Staples & Charles Ltd*       *Design: Ramona Ryabik with Robert Staples*
*225 North Fairfax Street*    *Photography: Gary Lee Super and others*
*Alexandria VA 22314-2694*    *Typeset in Adobe Garamond and Frutiger*
*1-800-544-1026*              *Printed by Oddi Printing Corp.*

*Library of Congress Catalog Card Number: 94-115104*

*Cover: **Season's Greetings** by Haddon H. Sundblom, 1962.
Title page: **The pause that refreshes** by Haddon H. Sundblom, 1953.
All illustrations, unless otherwise noted, are from the Archives of The
Coca-Cola Company.*

*Printed in Iceland*

*Display cutout based on **"They remembered me"** by Haddon H. Sundblom, 1942.*

# Preface

By virtually any measure, Coca-Cola is the most recognized and widely enjoyed product in the world—the universal pause that refreshes. At The Coca-Cola Company we believe that the flavor of Coca-Cola sets it apart from other soft drinks; but we also know that for more than one hundred years our advertising has captured the public's fancy and endeared Coca-Cola to generations of consumers.

In the 1920s, The Coca-Cola Company began to adopt Santa Claus as a salesman for the idea that "thirst knows no season" and thus, that wintertime is as good a time as summer for drinking Coca-Cola. Several artists tried their hand at illustrating Santa, but none quite captured his spirit until 1931 when American illustrator Haddon Sundblom put his brush to canvas and painted a new rendition. The "jolly old elf" must have liked what he saw because he came back year after year. Worldwide, the public embraced what they saw, and Haddon Sundblom's vision became everybody's vision. What started as an advertising campaign soon became a tradition.

Haddon Sundblom created hundreds of enduring advertising images for The Coca-Cola Company, but none has had the impact of his Santa Claus series. For over three decades, Sundblom's interpretations became etched in the American mind as the definitive characterization of Santa Claus. Sundblom's original oil paintings represent a legacy that goes far beyond that of an influential advertising campaign.

Over the past several Christmas seasons, through a series of exhibitions, The Coca-Cola Company has been sharing this rich collection of original art with consumers in the United States, Canada, and Japan. This publication presents that art for the first time in a format that provides historical perspective on Sundblom's work while emphasizing his creative genius. It is a catalogue that delights the eyes and evokes the same warm feelings about Santa and the spirit of Christmas that Sundblom took such pains to develop. We are indebted to Staples & Charles for their creativity in producing such a fitting tribute to this master of commercial illustration.

—— *Philip F. Mooney*
*Archivist*
*The Coca-Cola Company*

**Good Boys and Girls** *by Haddon H. Sundblom, 1951.*

## Who is Santa Claus?

Among the predecessors of Santa Claus, the most celebrated was St. Nicholas of Myra. His legend, revered by millions over a span of centuries, is apparently just that—a legend. There is no evidence that Nicholas ever existed, though he was long believed to have been born in A.D. 270 in Patara (once a port in Turkey), to have become Bishop of nearby Myra (now known as Kale), and after performing many miracles and acts of charity, to have died in 343 on December 6, ever since then his feast day.

Nicholas's good works were often done secretly and on behalf of the young. When three sisters reached marriageable age without enough money between them to make up even one dowry, Nicholas secretly gave them three bags of gold. The bags may have been the antecedents of the Christmas stocking, although in one version of this tale, the gold was thrown down the chimney of the girls' home and into a stocking hung there to dry.

After his canonization in the ninth century, veneration of Nicholas spread until he was perhaps the favorite saint in the calendar, with thousands of churches dedicated to him throughout Europe. His shrine, moved to Bari, Italy, as Turkey came under Moslem control late in the eleventh century, became one of the most popular pilgrimage sites.

At this time Christianity was becoming Europe's dominant religion, gaining converts by blending with the existing religious heritage of each area. Many saints took on attributes of local gods, and Christian holy days merged with harvest festivals and winter-solstice celebrations, some of which had existed for thousands of years. The most famous such celebration was the Roman Saturnalia, a week of eating, drinking, gambling, wearing of costumes, and giving of gifts, including branches cut from trees in a sacred wood. (These tokens of esteem would in Christmas custom become the switches left to punish "bad boys and girls.") Farther north, white-bearded Odin, principal diety of old northern Europe, was thought to roam the earth with other gods to punish evildoers during the week-plus December celebration of Jul; gifts of food were left overnight to feed the gods' horses and appease their vengeful riders.

By the late Middle Ages, the Christmas season as such was found across Europe, usually as part of a long and often raucous December festival. More charitable observances began; thirteenth-century French nuns marked Nicholas Eve by leaving food at the doors of the poor. This practice spread, followed logically—for Nicholas was the patron saint of children—by present-giving to children whose

**Saint Nicholas** *by Hans Sebald Beham (1500–1550), pen and black ink on paper. (Ailsa Mellon Bruce Fund, © 1992 National Gallery of Art, Washington D.C.)*

parents explained that the saint had ridden by in the night, leaving coveted treats.

With the coming of the Protestant Reformation in the sixteenth century, Catholic Nicholas was abandoned by newly Protestant believers and regimes. In Germany and elsewhere, Nicholas the gift-giver was replaced by a child—in German, the Christkindlein—first conceived as an incarnation of the infant Jesus. Soon, however, the Christkindlein began to travel with Nicholas looka-likes with other names, such as Père Nöel in France. And a third figure also began to appear. In central Europe, the Christkindlein often had a dwarfish helper: his many names included Hans Trapp, Knecht Ruprecht, Ru Klas, and Pelznickel (or, Nicholas in furs). Some of these simply assisted in delivering gifts; more often, they were mischievous, even demonic, and said to punish bad children with a sudden, frightening appearance or with such "gifts" as switches for whippings; the truly incorrigible could be threatened with kidnap-ping. In Holland and Flanders, the Christkindlein did not replace Nicholas, who still used his own name—in Dutch, Sinterklaas. His helper was Zwarte Piet ("Black Peter"), a name that was also a Dutch term for the devil.

In early colonial America, the Reformation made Christmas controversial, particularly in Puritan New England. In 1647, the English Parliament abolished the holiday. In 1659, even as the Puritan revolution unravelled, Massachusetts (mostly settled by Puritans fleeing harassment in the 1630s) set a fine for those who did not work on "such days as Christmas," and this regulation stood until 1881.

Farther south, English colonists loyal to the Church of England celebrated Christmas wherever they settled, with a morning religious service followed by parties, hearty dinners, caroling, and merriment. For the Dutch, who held their New Amsterdam colony from 1626 until the English took it over in 1664, Christmas was less important than December 6, Nicholas Day, which was in turn less prominent than it once had been in Holland.

Nevertheless in 1809, Washington Irving (1783–1859) published *A History of New York . . . by Diedrich Knickerbocker,* a gentle satire that invented much about New Amsterdam and exaggerated St. Nicholas's public presence there. Irving's wit was directed less at New York's Dutch past than at his peers, who in 1804 founded the New-York Historical Society with Nicholas as its patron saint. Early American patriots chose Nicholas as a symbol because in colonial America Holland was thought the most democratic of all countries. With the new nation established, the Society's members revived another Dutch tradition, Nicholas's role as a gift-bringer. In 1810, for their annual St. Nicholas day dinner—on Irving's first anniversary as a member—they printed a new woodcut of a traditional-looking Nicholas—tall, and wearing long robes—with a Dutch rhyme about "Sancte Claus."

By 1812, Irving had revised *Knickerbocker's History,* adding even more about Nicholas, described as "riding over the tops of the trees, in that selfsame waggon wherein he brings his yearly presents to children." Landing in the countryside to smoke his pipe, Nicholas then "twisted it in his hat-band, and laying his finger beside his nose . . . he returned over the tree-tops and disappeared." In 1821 the New York printer William Gilley issued another poem, with a "Santeclaus" who drove not a "waggon" but a sleigh drawn by one reindeer (new to Nicholas lore, and never explained), and was dressed all in fur, including a hat half his height. "Sante" Nicholas, tall in the Historical Society woodcut, had somehow become very short.

One of Gilley's friends embroidered this new figure in another and more magical poem. The family of Clement Clarke Moore (1779–1863) had lived in the New York area for more than a century; his was the third generation to occupy a hundred-acre farm in what is now downtown Manhattan, where he wrote on various subjects, produced a Hebrew dictionary, and finally became a faculty member at the General Theological Seminary. By commonly accepted legend, Moore wrote his famous verses on the day before Christmas of 1822, and read them to his six children (three more were

'Twas the night before Christmas, when all through the house

Not a creature was stirring, not even a mouse;

The stockings were hung by the chimney with care,

In hopes that St. Nicholas soon would be there;

The children were nestled all snug in their beds,

While visions of sugar-plums danced in their heads;

And Mamma in her 'kerchief, and I in my cap,

Had just settled our brains for a long winter's nap;

When out on the lawn there arose such a clatter,

I sprang from the bed to see what was the matter.

Away to the window I flew like a flash,

Tore open the shutters and threw up the sash.

The moon, on the breast of the new fallen snow,

Gave the lustre of mid-day to objects below,

When, what to my wondering eyes should appear,

But a miniature sleigh, and eight tiny rein-deer,

With a little old driver, so lively and quick,

I knew in a moment it must be St. Nick.

More rapid than eagles his coursers they came,

And he whistled, and shouted, and called them by name;

"Now, Dasher! now, Dancer! now, Prancer and Vixen!

On, Comet! on, Cupid! on, Donder and Blitzen!

To the top of the porch! to the top of the wall!

Now dash away! dash away! dash away all!"

As dry leaves that before the wild hurricane fly,

When they meet with an obstacle, mount to the sky;

So up to the house-top the coursers they flew,

With the sleigh full of Toys, and St. Nicholas too.

And then, in a twinkling, I heard on the roof

The prancing and pawing of each little hoof—

As I drew in my head, and was turning around,

Down the chimney St. Nicholas came with a bound.

He was dressed all in fur, from his head to his foot,

And his clothes were all tarnished with ashes and soot;

A bundle of Toys he had flung on his back,

And he look'd like a pedlar just opening his pack.

His eyes—how they twinkled! his dimples how merry!

His cheeks were like roses, his nose like a cherry!

His droll little mouth was drawn up like a bow,

And the beard of his chin was as white as the snow;

The stump of a pipe he held tight in his teeth,

And the smoke it encircled his head like a wreath;

He had a broad face and a little round belly

That shook, when he laughed, like a bowl full of jelly.

He was chubby and plump, a right jolly old elf,

And I laughed, when I saw him, in spite of myself;

A wink of his eye and a twist of his head,

Soon gave me to know I had nothing to dread;

He spoke not a word, but went straight to his work,

And fill'd all the stockings; then turned with a jerk,

And laying his finger aside of his nose,

And giving a nod, up the chimney he rose;

He sprang to his sleigh, to his team gave a whistle,

And away they all flew like the down of a thistle.

But I heard him exclaim, ere he drove out of sight,

"Happy Christmas to all, and to all a good night."

——Clement Clarke Moore, 1822.

*Illustration by F.O.C. Darley (1822–1888) for* A Visit from Saint Nicholas, *published by James G. Gregory, New York [1862]. (Archives Center, National Museum of American History, Smithsonian Institution)*

yet to come) after the evening's dinner. Soon after, a relative copied the poem and took it to nearby Troy, where on December 23, 1823, the editor of the *Troy Sentinel* published it anonymously as "An Account of a Visit from St. Nicholas." Within a year it was reprinted in New Jersey and Pennsylvania. Many uncredited publications later, Moore let his name appear with his verse in *The New-York Book of Poetry,* an 1837 anthology.

If Moore did not invent very much of his "St. Nick," he wrote of him vividly, devised his entrance by the chimney, and gave him a memorably named team of eight reindeer. From 1830 on, artists up to and including F.O.C. Darley, the first prominent American illustrator, depicted Santa Claus within guidelines Moore had created.

Moore's portrait of an "elf" in fur garments resembled the mythical Pelznickel, not found in New York but brought to nearby Pennsylvania by eighteenth-century German immigrants from the Palatinate-Rhineland region, where the Christmas tree also had originated. In the 1820s real-life Belsnickles (as they were called in German-American dialect) were at work across the southeast of Pennsylvania. The Belsnickle—an adult in furry disguise, with false whiskers as needed—would visit while children were still awake, put on a scary

performance, and depart; children's gifts, found the next morning, were credited to the Christkindlein, who had come while all were asleep.

With time, the visible Belsnickle began to overshadow the invisible Christkindlein and usurp its present-bringing. In an English-speaking society the Christkindlein's name melted into "Kriss Kringle." The two became confused with one another, and with Nicholas, and with the emerging Santa. The New Yorkers who devised Santa Claus simply adopted the Belsnickle image, making it more cheerful. In 1841, Philadelphia merchant J.W. Parkinson borrowed back the friendlier image and created a new twist by hiring a man in "Criscringle" garb to descend the outside of a chimney at his shop. Ever since, man-sized Kriss Kringles and Santas have appeared before delighted children, breaking down the idea of the elf-Santa.

The parents of Thomas Nast brought him to New York at the age of six from Landau, his birthplace in the German Palatinate. By 1862 he earned a staff position on *Harper's Weekly,* the nation's foremost illustrated paper, where he became a brutal and unsparing caricaturist, the terror of the American political class through the 1870s. Beginning in 1863, the subject of Santa Claus became a yearly working vacation from Nast's preoccupation with human folly. Over the next few years, Nast developed his personal image of Santa. In Moore, "the beard of his chin was as white as the snow"; Nast created a flowing set of whiskers, and dressed Santa "all in fur, from his head to his foot," in reference either to Moore, or to his own childhood memories of the German Pelznickel. For Christmas 1866, Nast drew a *Harper's* montage, "Santa Claus and His Works," with images that expanded Santa's legend to include the making of toys. McLoughlin Brothers, a publisher of children's books, approached Nast for new versions of these drawings. The resulting book appeared around 1869, with the same title and a poem by George P. Webster that placed Santa's home at the North Pole for the first time. The *Works* book, and a Nast/McLoughlin edition of the Moore poem, spread Nast's vision of Santa for decades. Though Nast created Santas until his break with *Harper's* in 1886, he did not quite establish his Santa as an archetype. He never settled on Santa's size, which changed to fit his fantasies. The enduring aspects of his Santa—billowing white beard, powerful pear-shaped physique, and sunny demeanor, all seen in "Merry Old Santa Claus" (1881)—gradually gained acceptance as essentials of all Santas, but in one major respect—their close-

**Merry Old Santa Claus** *by Thomas Nast (1840–1902), published in* Harper's Weekly, *January 1, 1881. (Staples & Charles, Washington D.C.)*

*Christmas card published by L. Prang & Co., Boston, 1886.*
*(Dede Schaeffer, Lancaster, Pennsylvania)*

fitting suits of fur—Nast's Santas would lose the battle of history.

By the late nineteenth century Santa Claus was everywhere, in magazines and newspapers, in children's books and board games, in songs and plays, as a doll and as a tree ornament. He also became a leading citizen of the growing world of advertising—in periodicals, on signs, on calendars and tradesmens' cards, and every other marketing medium of the day. These Santas were large and small, usually round but sometimes not, and wore either the Belsnickle furs or cloth suits of blue, red,

green, or even purple. Boston printer Louis Prang, like Nast an immigrant from Germany, had introduced to Americans the English custom of the Christmas card; Santa made an obvious subject for these, and in 1885 Prang issued a red-suited image that apparently sold unusually well, since two more red-suited Santas followed it in 1886. From this point on the red suit became more and more standard. Department-store Santas, Santas who stood on the streets to collect money for charities, even mail-order firms (which by the 1910s were providing inexpensive red-with-white-trim costumes for home use) all fell in line with the red-suited Santas of Prang, speeding the decline of the Belsnickle image and the multicolored Santas that followed it.

By the 1920s not every Santa wore red, but *The New York Times* gave a fair picture of Santa as of November 27, 1927: "A standardized Santa Claus appears to New York children. Height, weight, stature are almost exactly standardized, as are the red garments, the hood and the white whiskers. The pack full of toys, ruddy cheeks and nose, bushy eyebrows and a jolly, paunchy effect are also inevitable parts of the requisite make-up."

"Standardized..." "Inevitable..." It was this image which a young commercial artist would refresh from 1931 on.

*Concept sketch for painting by Haddon H. Sundblom. The final painting for 1964 was developed from this charcoal drawing. (Marshall Lane, Atlanta, Georgia)*

# Haddon H. Sundblom (1899–1976)

Born in Muskegon, Michigan, on June 22, 1899, Haddon Hubbard Sundblom struck out for Chicago soon after his mother died when he was only thirteen. For seven years he worked construction jobs by day while studying by night, at first intending to become an architect. During a layoff, he decided to become an illustrator, and began his new career in 1920 as an office boy at the Charles Everett Johnson Studios, one of Chicago's largest. By 1925, Sundblom and two colleagues had started their own firm.

In the 1920s, Chicago's advertising community was the nation's most vital, and Sundblom was among its more vital presences. Standing three inches over six feet, he had a booming voice, a personality others called jovial (he called it argumentative), and many clients. He painted for Cream of Wheat and Nabisco Shredded Wheat cereals, Aunt Jemima pancake mix, Maxwell House coffee, Palmolive, Cashmere Bouquet and Camay soaps, Whitman chocolates, Goodyear tires, Four Roses whiskey, Budweiser, Schlitz, Lone Star and Pabst beers, the U.S. Marine Corps, and many car makers, including Ford, Packard, Lincoln, Buick, Pierce-Arrow, and Jordan. He also illustrated fiction for *The Saturday Evening Post, Ladies' Home Journal, Cosmopolitan,* and *Good Housekeeping.*

The Coca-Cola Company was among Sundblom's earliest clients. In 1924 he made his first sketch and by the next year was at work on the advertising campaign for 1926. At that time The Coca-Cola Company was hiring many of America's premier illustrators—Frederic Mizen, Hayden Hayden, Norman Rockwell, N.C. Wyeth, Bradshaw Crandell—to create ads. Sundblom would become the Company's most prolific artist, treating subjects that ranged from bathing beauties to soda-fountain scenes. During his peak period in the 1940s, he would produce at least half of all billboard art for advertising Coca-Cola.

*The inaugural Sundblom Santa watches over staff and salesmen standing in front of the Coca-Cola Bottling Company in Memphis, Tennessee, 1931.*

There's this about Coke...

**"It's my gift for thirst"**

Leave it to old Santa —he knows the importance of choosing Christmas presents to fit the occasion. He knows something about refreshment, too. This merry world traveler could tell you that ice-cold Coca-Cola is the perfect gift for thirst —in Mombasa, in Rome, in Rio ... or where you live.

Drink Coca-Cola

See EDDIE FISHER on "Coke Time" NBC Television twice each week.

*Magazine advertisement based on* **"It's my gift for thirst"** *by Haddon H. Sundblom, 1954.*

From 1931 on, Haddon Sundblom created at least one painting of Santa Claus annually for The Coca-Cola Company. The series would stretch across a third of a century, in part because of the strength of Sundblom's vision. Disliking the cheap costumes and meager look common to department-store and charity Santas, Sundblom countered with abundance—a lavish use of fur and leather (belt, boots, and gloves were all massive), a billowing beard, and a waistline so ample it required a belt and suspenders. Santa as seen by Sundblom provided an image that fit perfectly, a sense of instant recognition that glowed with warmth and overwhelmed disbelief. By 1940, The Coca-Cola Company was, in its own words, "the outstanding poster [i.e., billboard] advertiser in the country," ensuring massive exposure for the yearly Santa, who also appeared in a blizzard of magazine ads and other media. Though Haddon Sundblom was all but unknown beyond his profession, his generous and quite personal conception was everywhere.

According to Marshall Lane, who worked on advertising for The Coca-Cola Company from 1937 to 1971, the preparation of each year's Santa began within weeks of the preceding Christmas. At least one painting, for the poster campaign, had to be ready by early spring. (In nearly every year from 1944 to 1953, there were two or even three Santa paintings—one for billboards, one for magazines, and sometimes another for point-of-sale items.) Creative director Archie Lee and others at D'Arcy (the St. Louis-based advertising agency that held the Coca-Cola account from 1906 to 1956) developed underlying concepts as line drawings, trying to maintain continuity of feeling and image from previous years. Discussions involving Sundblom,

Lee, and Lane led to Sundblom's own sketches, followed by his rough color version. Once approved, this became his basis for posing his models—live, in the 1930s, or in photographs thereafter. His first model for Santa was his friend Lou Prentice, a retired salesman; after Prentice's death, Sundblom found his Santa model in the mirror.

A fast painter, Sundblom completed each canvas in one or two sittings, working in a loose, painterly style. Still, with all the demands on his time, D'Arcy and The Coca-Cola Company had to cajole him to meet deadlines. Beginning in the early 1950s, by using dye transfers to add various elements created by others, adjustments were often made for point-of-sale displays. By the early 1960s, the formats of the paintings were analyzed for multiple uses—for vertical print ads and horizontal billboards especially—before approval. Now one painting could serve all purposes. Though his late Santas were not in the style Sundblom preferred, they kept the buoyancy of earlier editions. Sundblom was a professional, though in a profession that was changing and shrinking.

By the 1960s television was in nearly every American home, and ad agencies shifted more of their budgets to the newer medium. Photography almost drove illustration out of magazine advertis-

In 1964 Haddon H. Sundblom submitted his last paintings of Santa Claus for consideration by the advertising department of The Coca-Cola Company. The one to his right was used for that year's Christmas campaign. The one to his left was not adopted until 1966. The whereabouts of the 1966 original painting is unknown.

ing, and the large-format magazines that could do the most justice to quality illustrations—*Collier's, Life, The Saturday Evening Post*—were disappearing. Billboards came under increasing state and local restriction, as well as the limitations of the federal Highway Beautification Act of 1965.

Sundblom created his last two Santas for The Coca-Cola Company in 1964, then continued his career at a semi-retired pace until his death in 1976; he painted on commission from private collectors, and in his last years received acclaim from the general-interest press that he had previously known only from trade publications.

**17**

## "Away with a tired thirsty face"

While it may be a modern conceit that a tired person is not "normal," masks have been a part of Christmas and its predecessors for thousands of years. Father Christmas, another of Santa's many predecessors, was known as "Old Christmas" when he first appeared in English folk plays at the end of the Middle Ages. An 1846 set of stage directions for one such play presented at Cornwall, England, described him as wearing a mask, as well as a long white wig.

In the United States of 1933, seasonal professional Santas were common; department stores hired them to greet children, and charities stationed them on sidewalks to collect donations. For the amateur, standard Santa costumes were readily available. Montgomery Ward, for example, offered one for less than four dollars, while for a similar price Sears sold a different style with jacket and trousers, instead of the one-piece robe and "imitation leather leggings" of the Ward suit; both were red with white trim. Either firm would provide a Santa mask, complete with white beard and red hood, for less than a dollar.

*"Away with a tired thirsty face"* by Haddon H. Sundblom, 1933
*Oil on canvas, 32" x 62" (81cm x 157cm)*

## The pause that keeps you going

Sundblom's 1931 Santa was not "all in fur," nor would anyone call his belly little. Judging from his proportion to the glass of Coca-Cola, he was no elf. Otherwise he was much in keeping with the letter of Clement Clarke Moore's creation, and even more significantly, with its spirit. This edition, re-painted in 1934, added a couple of traditional touches. Bare-headed in 1931, Santa now wears a fur-trimmed hat, and one of his cuffs seems "tarnished with ashes and soot," as in "A Visit from St. Nicholas."

Though Moore's St. Nick controlled his reindeer with whistles and shouts alone—even reins were not mentioned—in the horse-drawn world of the nineteenth century, whips understandably found their way into many Santa portrayals; the Pennsylvania-German tradition of the Belsnickle, a costumed, masked figure who visited homes and threatened children with whippings, also probably weighed on some of these illustrations. But while this Sundblom Santa carried a whip to speed up his deliveries, he did not carry the switches that the traditional Santa supposedly leaves for "bad boys and girls."

**The pause that keeps you going** by Haddon H. Sundblom, 1934
(Originally painted in 1931; modified for 1934 advertising campaign.)
Oil on canvas, 34" x 47" (86cm x 109cm)

## "Me too"

The worldwide Depression affected Americans throughout the 1930s, but in 1936 the American economy surged forward as it had not done since late in the 1920s. The Depression was far from over, but under temporarily improving conditions Santa the present-bringer could be portrayed enjoying himself in the midst of the bounty of his own toys without risking resentment from too many consumer-parents in tight circumstances. The selection of presents around him meets many needs: for the girls, a doll in the Shirley Temple style evokes the child movie star of the moment; for the boys, an electric train provides something to share and enjoy with their father; and for the baby of the family, a pull-toy baby duck quacks cheerfully.

**"Me too"** *by Haddon H. Sundblom, 1936*
*Oil on canvas, 33" x 65" (84cm x 165cm)*

## "Give and take," say I

The economic recovery of 1936 dissolved in 1937, but ads for Coca-Cola continued to emphasize America's drive toward prosperity. Not only is the raided refrigerator filled with Coca-Cola and lots of food, including a traditional Christmas turkey, it *is* a refrigerator, as opposed to the iceboxes still used in most U.S. households in 1937. Though often interested in promoting Coca-Cola as a mealtime drink—in this period, when visits to restaurants were beyond most pocketbooks, a how-to booklet entitled "When You Entertain" was offered to customers for ten cents—The Coca-Cola Company rarely enlisted Santa in these efforts by showing him eating; this is the only overt example.

**"Give and take," say I** *by Haddon H. Sundblom, 1937*
*Oil on canvas, 35" x 65" (90cm x 165cm)*

## "Thanks for *the pause that refreshes*"

Children are the focus of the contemporary Christmas, and evidences of children abound in the Santas for Coca-Cola in the '30s and '40s, but since children are usually asleep when Santa arrives, only here can a child be seen. A charming child it is, softly lit from the "firelight" angle common in Sundblom's early Santas, and with the serene quality he brought to his short-story illustration assignments in the 1920s. By this time the immensely successful campaign—"The Pause That Refreshes"—was ten years old; and as any parent knows, the love of a child can be a most wonderful pause, and one that refreshes more than any drink.

*"Thanks for **the pause that refreshes**" by Haddon H. Sundblom, 1938*
*Oil on canvas, 32" x 62" (81cm x 157cm)*

## "Somebody knew I was coming"

The Coca-Cola Company's advertising nearly always emphasized a red sign with white lettering, typically on a field of green. Yellow was added for accents, and was the color of the cases for bottles. In the Santa paintings, lettering is usually yellow on a green background or white on red. The universal adoption for twentieth-century Santas of a white-fur-trimmed red suit—replacing Clement Clarke Moore's description "dressed all in fur" and Thomas Nast's furry union suit—made him a perfect spokesman for the perfect pause. In this classic example, ermine fur and his own snow-white hair and beard frame his rosy cheeks, his cherry-like nose, and the broad red expanse of his chest.

*"Somebody knew I was coming"* by Haddon H. Sundblom, 1940
*Oil on canvas, 26" x 44" (66cm x 112cm)*

## "They remembered *me*"

This was Sundblom's first full-length standing Santa, and therefore the first of what would become a long series of stand-up Santa display cutouts— nearly life-size cardboard figures that could be used face-to-face with customers in grocery stores and at other points of sale. More than many of Sundblom's creations, this Santa is clearly engaged in his rounds. Having apparently walked through drifts of "new fallen snow" (and tracked some of it through the living room), he takes a seemingly much-needed break before a grandfather clock that marks an appropriately wee hour of the morning.

*"They remembered **me**" by Haddon H. Sundblom, 1942*
*Oil on canvas, 51" x 51" (130cm x 130cm)*

## "Wherever I go . . ."

By the end of the 1930s Santa had worked so hard that he needed to relax—and relax he did, in a comfortable overstuffed chair, big enough for his sizeable frame. In the original 1939 painting, used in advertisements with the slogan "And the same to you," Santa offers a bottle of Coca-Cola to potentially equally tired viewers, urging them to relax from rounds of chores as he does with a refreshing drink. When the painting was altered for the 1943 advertising campaign, Santa's left hand was moved downward to hold a child's note to "Dear Santa," and the bottle of Coca-Cola was transformed into Santa's own reward.

*"Wherever I go . . ." by Haddon H. Sundblom, 1943*
*(Originally painted in 1939; modified for the 1943 advertising campaign.)*
*Oil on canvas, 31" x 55" (79cm x 140cm)*

**"Merry Christmas to you."**

Here is another full-length standing Santa, a vertical image ideal for point-of-sale display pieces. Such displays usually came in several sizes; in 1944, one was 54″ (137 cm) tall to stand in a window or on the floor, and and another was 14″ (36 cm) high for placement on counters or merchandise. Bottlers would buy sets—one each of large and small—for less than a dollar per set to give to stores in their territory. Although Santa's double handful of six bottles promoted the purchase of Coca-Cola in quantity, wartime sugar rationing limited the supply, and a shortage of cardboard made the familiar six-pack unavailable.

**"Merry Christmas to you."** *by Haddon H. Sundblom, 1944*
*Oil on canvas, 40" x 29" (102cm x 74cm)*

## "They knew what I wanted"

With the end of the Second World War came demobilization, return to civilian life, and home-comings around the world. There were the joys of celebrating the holidays—with family and friends, for the first time in several years—and the anxieties of resuming lives so abruptly interrupted. Still, for Americans, who in December 1945 would see the billboard based on this painting more often than any other billboard, Santa Claus and Coca-Cola offered a comforting vision of return to a warm and welcoming home. For all too many others around the world, the upheavals of the war meant starting anew.

**"They knew what I wanted"** *by Haddon H. Sundblom, 1945*
*Oil on canvas, 26" x 45" (66cm x 114cm)*

## Greetings

No one knows when children began writing letters to Santa, but certainly the practice was common by the 1870s. Though Santa's clothing and reindeer-powered transportation implied residence in a cold climate, he was not established at the North Pole until the McLoughlin Brothers published *Santa Claus and His Works* (circa 1869), with illustrations by Thomas Nast and a poem by George P. Webster:

*In a nice little city called Santa Claus-ville,*
*With its houses and church at the foot of the hill*
*Lives jolly old Santa Claus . . .*
*His home through the long summer months,*
    *you must know,*
*Is near the North Pole, in the ice and snow . . .*

Apart from the North Pole, childrens' letters were (and are) sometimes addressed to nearby cities, or to "Heaven," or simply to "Santa Claus" in a variety of creative spellings. Since the 1890s their numbers have substantially increased the duties of U.S. postal workers, who could not hope to improve on the now discarded custom of parents' "mailing" letters up the chimney on the draft of a roaring fire—with the children looking on, of course.

**Greetings** *by Haddon H. Sundblom, 1945*
*Oil on canvas, 49" x 34" (124cm x 86cm)*

## For me

This bottle of Coca-Cola, tied with a bow, is quickly recognized as a gift for Santa Claus. Fancy wrapping papers and ribbons are a twentieth century tradition, but red ribbons at Christmas have a long heritage. In 1741, members of the Moravian Church settled in Bethlehem, Pennsylvania. A diary (kept in German) recorded all of the Bethlehem Church's Christmas services from 1742 on, including the second of four services in December 1756:

*At eight o'clock, the children assembled . . . [after a number of hymns and an address from one of the adults] they received each a gift with reminder of the greatest and most wonderful gift when the Savior presented Himself to us. And, at last, each received a wax candle, lighted while hymn stanzas were being sung, and before one was aware of it more than 250 candles were ablaze, producing a charming effect . . . Then they went happily homeward . . . The girls, however, met once more and received, during the singing of a hymn, new red ribbons for their caps, which, also, occasioned not a little joy.*

**For me** *by Haddon H. Sundblom, 1946*
*Oil on canvas, 18" x 35" (46cm x 89cm)*

## Busy man's pause

Brush behind ear, paint pots at elbow, and bottle in hand, this is the first view of Haddon Sundblom's Santa in his workshop. Clement Clarke Moore never mentions the source of the "bundle of toys" brought by his Santa, who seemingly worked only one night per year. But Santa gained year-round employment and a workshop with elfin helpers in later works, including the anonymously written 1859 *Harper's Weekly* poem, "The Wonders of Santa Claus":

*In his house upon the top of a hill,*
*And almost out of sight,*
*He keeps a great many elves at work,*
*All working with all their might,*
*To make a million of pretty things,*
*Cakes, sugar-plums, and toys,*
*To fill the stockings, hung up you know*
*By the little girls and boys."*

The workshop gained great popularity in the McLoughlin-published *Santa Claus and His Works;* in Thomas Nast's illustrations, the elves are absent and Santa busies himself in his workshop making toys, or in his parlor sewing clothes for the dolls.

**Busy man's pause** *by Haddon H. Sundblom, 1947*
*Oil on canvas, 28" x 50" (71cm x 127cm)*

## Hospitality

Once again, Santa stops during his rounds to enjoy a refreshing glass of Coca-Cola, this time dropping his bag of toys on a chair. Holly, here tucked in Santa's hat, is a tradition preceding Christmas itself; branches of the spiny-leafed plant with tiny red fruit were exchanged as tokens of friendship by Romans during the winter festival of Saturnalia. Sundblom may have adapted this decorated headgear from Thomas Nast, who adorned the caps of many of his Santas with a holly sprig.

**Hospitality** *by Haddon H. Sundblom, 1948*
*Oil on canvas, 50" x 33" (127cm x 84cm)*

## Travel *refreshed*

*When, what to my wondering eyes should appear,*
*But a miniature sleigh, and eight tiny rein-deer,*
*With a little old driver, so lively and quick,*
*I knew in a moment it must St. Nick.*
*More rapid than eagles his coursers they came,*
*And he whistled, and shouted, and called them by name;*
*"Now, Dasher! now, Dancer! now, Prancer and Vixen!*
*On, Comet! on, Cupid! on, Donder and Blitzen!*
*To the top of the porch! to the top of the wall!*
*Now dash away! dash away! dash away all!"*

Although this painting does not clearly show eight reindeer, its reference to the well-known team from Clement Clarke Moore's poem is obvious. What remains unclear is why reindeer became associated with the 1820s Santas of Moore and his predecessor William Gilley, a printer who in 1821 published *A New-Year's Present, to the Little Ones from Five to Twelve,* with a poem that began "Old Santeclaus with much delight, His reindeer drives this frosty night. . . ." No other element of the Santa legend is quite so mysterious. Appropriately, if coincidentally, Sundblom's Santas for 1949 are themselves rather mysterious in tone.

**Travel *refreshed*** *by Haddon H. Sundblom, 1949*
*Oil on canvas, 26" x 46" (66cm x 117cm)*

## Travel refreshed

The 1949 Sundblom Christmas paintings include not only Santa but also Sundblom's other enduring creation, the "Sprite Boy," who was originally used in 1942 to introduce the name "Coke," and to remind the public to use the brand names "Coke" or "Coca-Cola" or when asking for their favorite soft drink. Sundblom later described the birth of "Sprite Boy," who "was born wearing a soda jerk's cap, but we soon fitted him with a nice bottle cap which he wears most of the time. Archie Lee was his "father," but he doesn't resemble him at all. He has my daughter's eyes and my mouth—I know, I'm his mother!" ("Sprite Boy" wore his soda jerk cap to promote fountain sales of Coke; he wore the bottle cap more frequently because of the larger market for the bottled beverage.)

Here, as in the previous painting, the "Sprite Boy" not only holds the reins of the team, but maintains eye contact with the viewer while Santa drinks from a bottle of Coca-Cola; this darker treatment, with Santa looming over the rest of the scene, is even more dreamlike. After 1949 "Sprite Boy" would not appear with Santa, and the youthful figure with the sparkling bow tie and prematurely white hair would be gradually phased out of advertising for Coca-Cola, disappearing altogether by 1958.

**Travel refreshed** *by Haddon H. Sundblom, 1949*
*Oil on canvas, 36" x 29" (91cm x 74cm)*

Travel refreshed

## "For Santa"

As in 1949, the paintings for 1950 are dominated by a "spirit" whose image overarches all; much of the Company's advertising for 1949 and '50 used stylistically similar images, such as landscapes dominated by skyscraper-sized vending machines. Otherwise, much has changed. Santa once again establishes eye contact with the viewer, and is one of only two main elements rather than three. The action figures are not galloping animals, but children filling the refrigerator in happy anticipation of a visit. Consistent lighting, sourced from the refrigerator, helps to cement the harmonious whole.

**"For Santa"** *by Haddon H. Sundblom, 1950*
*Oil on canvas, 24" x 43" (61cm x 109cm)*

## "For Santa"

By the 1950s Sundblom was wintering, though not vacationing, in Tucson, Arizona. The family next door included Lani and Sancy Nason, two sisters who became his models for paintings in 1950, 1952, and 1953. Sundblom commented: "I painted one of the sisters as a boy. I don't know whether she liked being a boy or not. I never asked her."

As early as the 1937 painting, Santa was browsing the refrigerator for Coca-Cola and food; now the children, knowing that he knows just where to find his reward, deliberately leave bottles of Coke there "For Santa."

*"**For Santa"** by Haddon H. Sundblom, 1950*
*Oil on canvas, 35" x 29" (89cm x 74cm)*

## Now it's my time

Although Lou Prentice, the retired salesman who was Sundblom's original Santa model, died in the late 1940s, photographs and memories of him probably continued to influence Sundblom's annual efforts. By the time he created this Santa, however, he had clearly become his own model. (Actually, he had always painted Santas using the shape of his own eyebrows, rather than Prentice's.) Sundblom painted his self-portraits from photographs, according to his wife, Betty, but even in such paintings he tended to assume the three-quarter-view angle common to artists who paint themselves from a mirror's reflection.

**Now it's my time** *by Haddon Sundblom, 1951*
*Oil on canvas, 25" x 35" (64cm x 89cm)*

Now it's my time

## Good Boys and Girls

Haddon Sundblom's wife Betty recalls that he did, at times, refer to the classic Santas Thomas Nast had created in the previous century. This 1951 Santa brings to mind Nast's "Santa Claus' Mail," published in 1871. In that drawing, Santa sits smoking his pipe between two piles of letters— "from naughty children's parents" (higher than the desk itself), and "from good children's parents" (a much smaller pile). Eighty years later, the pipe has been replaced by a bottle of Coca-Cola, and Santa's ledger lists only "Good Boys and Girls." Apparently, the bad kind no longer exist.

**Good Boys and Girls** *by Haddon H. Sundblom, 1951*
*Oil on canvas, 38" x 33" (97cm x 84cm)*

## ...the *gift* for thirst

There is a simple explanation for the unusually car-
toonish quality of the Santa in this painting for the
1952 billboard. This is not a finished painting, but
a rare example of a final Sundblom sketch, made
just before undertaking the painting itself, and for
approval by The Coca-Cola Company and its ad
agency, the D'Arcy Advertising Company of St.
Louis, Missouri. In the final billboard, the Nason
sisters (again painted as boy and girl) appeared
much as they do here, but the Santa more closely
resembled a reversed image of the painting on the
following pages.

**...the *gift* for thirst** *by Haddon H. Sundblom, 1952*
*Oil on canvas, 29" x 54" (74cm x 137cm)*

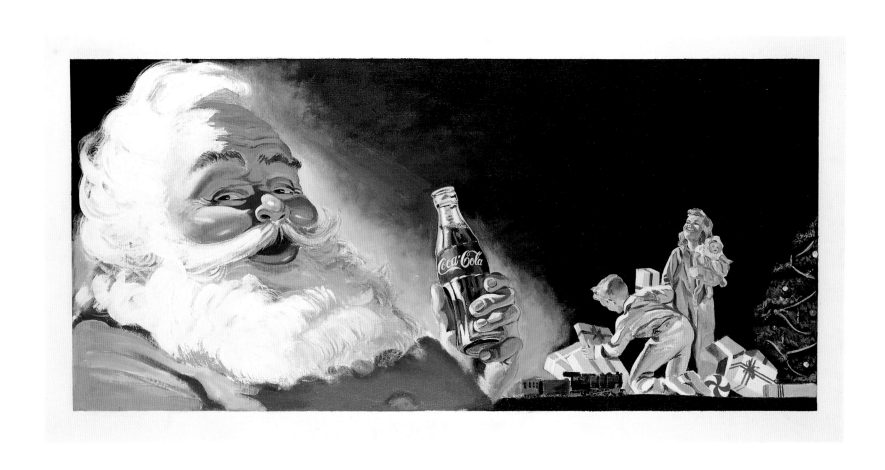

### . . . and now the *gift* for thirst

Though generally similar, the 1952 paintings admit differing interpretations. Both offer the first views of Christmas morning in the Sundblom series, with brother and sister opening presents (including, as in the 1936 painting, a doll and an electric train). Each also includes a giant Santa, out-sized compared to the children, pausing for refreshment at the completion of his rounds. Placement and perspective, however, alter our view; in this painting, the little girl seems to be thinking of Santa, while in the painting on the previous page, Santa's foreground position makes him appear to be thinking of the enjoyment he has brought.

**. . . and now the *gift* for thirst** *by Haddon H. Sundblom, 1952*
*Oil on canvas, 47" x 36" (119cm x 91cm)*

## The pause that *refreshes*

Children continued to flock to Sundblom's Santas, not as drinkers of Coke, but as good boys and girls offering a treat to a favorite elder.  The single bottle in this painting recalls an occasion years before, when The Coca-Cola Company withheld its approval from an advertising illustration of a young child serving Coca-Cola to her mother until one of the two bottles in the painting was removed—and with it, the implication that the child might also partake.

**The pause that *refreshes*** *by Haddon H. Sundblom, 1953*
*Oil on canvas, 28" x 50" (71cm x 127cm)*

## "It's my gift for thirst"

Very much at ease in his twenty-fourth year on the job, the 1954 Santa leaned casually against a wall— or against a single straight line in the magazine ad version (see page 16), designed in a modern style new to this series. So casual is this Santa that his characteristic broad belt is worn backwards. This tiny breach of convention had appeared in other Santas by Sundblom, but by 1954 the annual Sundblom Santa had many loyal and observant admirers who directed a stream of letters to the Company, proving that at times Santa is watched as closely as he watches others.

Sundblom, like Santa, may also have relaxed into his long-standing yearly assignment, but he would soon know that illustrators have less job security than legends.

**"It's my gift for thirst"** *by Haddon H. Sundblom, 1954*
*Oil on canvas, 42" x 34" (107cm x 86cm)*

## Almost everyone
## appreciates the best . . .

For The Coca-Cola Company, the mid-1950s were a time of relative turmoil and increasing competitive pressure from rival soft drinks, and a faint echo of this entered the Santa advertising for 1955. With hardly an exception, ads in the Archie Lee years had straightforwardly cited the virtues of Coca-Cola. The 1955 copy not only sounded a more uncertain note—why "*Almost* everyone"?—but also described Coca-Cola as "the best," raising the possibility of other choices. (Sundblom himself, in a 1955 letter, alluded to the choice Thomas Nast's Santa might have made: "[Santa Claus] seems much happier since he gave up the hard stuff and became a Coca-Cola convert.") Another competitive move in 1955 was the addition of larger bottle sizes (ten, twelve, and twenty-six ounces) though the bottle in this painting remains the traditional six-and-one-half-ounce model. The next major shift in the history of Coca-Cola would be a change of advertising agencies.

**Almost everyone appreciates the best . . .** *by Haddon H. Sundblom, 1955*
*Oil on canvas, 21" x 36" (53cm x 91cm)*

## For Sparkling Holidays

The original 1953 version of this Sundblom painting now exists only in various forms of paper ephemera, such as magazine ads and calendars. It included four elves, all hard at work on dolls, a rocking horse, a jack-in-the-box, and a toy train. This overpainted version was created in 1956, obscuring all the toys-in-progress from 1953 and all the elves, with the exception of one who was moved to the right and slightly up within the frame to put a finishing touch on the painting's title.

**For Sparkling Holidays** *by Haddon H. Sundblom, 1956*
*(Originally painted in 1953; modified for the 1956 advertising campaign.)*
*Oil on canvas, 40" x 32" (102cm x 81cm)*

## Santa's pause

This painting, probably created for the 1956 or 1957 Christmas campaigns, was initially passed over by McCann-Erickson, The Coca-Cola Company's new advertising agency, in favor of another treatment of the same concept by a different artist. With its companion piece on the following pages, this represents the last of Sundblom's Santas in what might be called his original classic style. Relaxing in shirt-sleeves at the North Pole at the completion of his yearly job well done, Santa peels off his boots, and is captured not cartoonishly but with realism, as if in a candid snapshot taken by one of his countless friends.

**Santa's pause** *by Haddon H. Sundblom, 1958*
*Oil on canvas, 26" x 46" (66cm x 117cm)*

## The Pause That Refreshes

Beneath the chair we see a fawn, too young for sleigh duty but an appropriate pet for Santa. Although this deer may have been intended to remind viewers of Bambi, the central figure of Walt Disney's 1942 children's movie, "the most famous reindeer of all" in the Santa Claus legend is, of course, Rudolph. In 1939, Robert L. May wrote a children's story about a deer whose odd attribute—a glowing nose—led first to rejection by Dasher *et al,* followed by heroic leadership of the entire team on a zero-visibility Christmas Eve. Montgomery Ward (May's employer) published the story as a children's book, with great success. Ten years later, Johnny Marks converted the story into a song. Gene Autry, singer and cowboy star of movies and television, had a 1947 hit with "Here Comes Santa Claus"; he chose "Rudolph, the Red-Nosed Reindeer" as a follow-up. The result was the best-selling record of his career, and the first of more than four hundred recorded Rudolphs.

**The Pause That Refreshes** *by Haddon H. Sundblom, 1958*
*Oil on canvas, 35" x 30" (89cm x 76cm)*

## Refreshing Surprise

Sundblom's late Santas differ from those of the 1930s, 1940s, and early 1950s not only in their more sharply defined painting style, but also in content. Most of the earlier paintings were essentially portraits, and Santa himself was their main subject. From 1959 onward, Santa was treated as one of several actors within a series of narrative scenes, and often upstaged (as here) by aggressively cute children or dogs. Compare this painting with any of those more naturally posed by the Nason sisters in the early 1950s, and the change will be obvious.

**Refreshing Surprise** *by Haddon H. Sundblom, 1959*
*Oil on canvas, 28" x 49" (71cm x 124cm)*

## A Merry Christmas calls for Coke

Though an entirely new piece, this painting recapitulates themes from two earlier Sundbloms. An elf pours Santa a glass of Coca-Coca, repeating the "being served" motif from the 1953 painting, "The pause that *refreshes*." The elves themselves—larger, younger, and clean-shaven—return from "For Sparkling Holidays" of 1956. (The "drum and bugle" elves at the painting's right were added to provide a location for the Coca-Cola logo on the billboard ad.) As in the 1958 paintings, Santa is rewarded for a job well done not only with the removal of his boots, but with a bottle of Coca-Cola. This time, however, he sits in a comfortable, old-fashioned armchair; the late Sundbloms grow more deliberately nostalgic, almost from one year to the next.

**A Merry Christmas calls for Coke** *by Haddon H. Sundblom, 1960*
*Oil on canvas (cutout and mounted on painted composite panel), 49" x 43" (124cm x 109cm)*

## When Friends drop in

Clement Clarke Moore's Santa borrowed a familiar but ambiguous gesture—"laying his finger aside of his nose"—from another American writer, Washington Irving. In 1809 Irving published *A History of New York . . . by Diedrich Knickerbocker,* a satirical and largely fictional work describing the Dutch colony of New Amsterdam, taken over and renamed New York by the English in 1664. Irving humorously exaggerated St. Nicholas's place in the history of the Dutch settlement, and in an 1812 revision of *Knickerbocker's History* he stretched things even further, adding a passage in which one settler dreams of Nicholas "riding over the tops of the trees, in that selfsame waggon wherein he brings his yearly presents to children." Nicholas lands to smoke his pipe, then "laying his finger beside his nose, gave the astonished Van Kortlandt [the settler] a very significant look, then mounting his waggon, he returned over the tree-tops and disappeared." The finger-laying of Moore's Santa has usually been seen as magical, allowing him to rise up the chimney, but Sundblom's Santa, shushing a yapping schnauzer to avoid waking a sleeping family, provides another possible interpretation.

**When Friends drop in** *by Haddon H. Sundblom, 1961*
*Oil on canvas, 40" x 37" (102cm x 94cm)*

## Season's Greetings

Most of the late Sundblom Santa paintings reinterpret earlier ideas, but with a style and spirit that were consistent and new. In these paintings, Santa retains his adult size, but displays an impish, childlike personality. And the later the Sundblom Santa, the earlier the idea revisited; here he reaches back to "Me too," from 1936. Just a big kid at heart, Santa plays amongst the toys he has just delivered. As in 1936, he has brought an electric train; this time, however, there is also a helicopter, something which did not exist until 1940.

**Season's Greetings** *by Haddon H. Sundblom, 1962*
*Oil on canvas, 40" x 39" (102cm x 99cm)*

## things go better with Coke

At the end of his tenure, Sundblom's Santa seems to have become a member of the family, rather than a visitor briefly welcomed once a year. Indeed, he almost seems to recede into the background, making way for attention to the children, their new dog, and the bottle of Coca-Cola. In 1961, a dog threatened to give away Santa's presence; now the dog becomes a gift, and no threat at all. (Sundblom on his canine model: "Actually, it's a gray poodle—but I painted it black because it had to stand out. I fuzzed up its coat a bit because I thought it would be cuter if it were a bundle of fuzz.") Holding one child on his lap, and both children in rapture over the bounty he has brought them, Santa Claus appears thoroughly content in the role of the ideal grandparent.

**things go better with Coke** *by Haddon H. Sundblom, 1964*
*Oil on canvas, 32" x 38" (81cm x 97cm)*

ISBN 0-9634907-0-2